THE COURAGE TO FEEL

THE COURAGE TO FEEL

A JOURNEY OF SELF DESCOVERY

Paul Garner

Sentir Press

The Courage To Feel Copyright © 2020 by Paul Garner. All Rights Reserved.

All rights reserved. No part of this book may be reproduced in any form or by any electronic or mechanical means including information storage and retrieval systems, without permission in writing from the author. The only exception is by a reviewer, who may quote short excerpts in a review.

Scripture quotations taken from The Holy Bible, New International Version® NIV® Copyright © 1973 1978 1984 2011 by Biblica, Inc. TM
Used by permission. All rights reserved worldwide.

Cover design by: Kirsty Elen Illustration
www.kirstyelen.com

Published by SENTIR PRESS the publishing arm of Paul Garner Counselling Services
www.paulgarnercounsellingservices.com

ISBN-13: 9798682974115

Contents

Acknowledgements 9
Preface 11
1. God desires truth in the inner being 17
2. Biology - what we know 23
3. How is it affecting John's & Jane's lives? 31
4. What it is to be human? 37
5. What it is to be spiritual? 43
6. What about the body? 49
7. Wrong use of Scripture 55
8. Looking back 61
9. What's in your glass? 67
10. The Mighty Dot. 73
11. Person Centred Counselling 81
12. Relationships 89
13. Stereotypes and prejudice 103
14. Free fall thinking 109
15. Start to live 113
16. Faith and feelings, the railway track 121
17. Structure, order & boundaries 129
18. Let's bring this to a close 137
About the author 141
Sources 143

Acknowledgements

Thank you to all of my friends that have encouraged me in the writing of this book, and to those who read it and gave me feedback. A special thanks to Joy who taught me grammar and made it readable, to Kathryn who helped with final proof reading, and to David for making it printable.

Many thanks and much respect to John Pettifor and David Shearman, who through the Training School and the many conferences and relational day's at The Christian Centre, Nottingham, played a large part in shaping my character as a church leader, husband and dad. Thank you for your support over the years and your kind words of recommendation for this book.

To the many people that I have met that have shaped my life, with some becoming lifelong friends. To my two sons, James and Jonathon, who have made me the very proud father that I am. Special thanks to my wife of forty one years, Dawn, as I would not be the man I am without her.

Above all to Jesus my Saviour who took a broken man, made him whole and filled him with purpose.

Preface

Why write this little book? Many great minds have written books regarding counselling and psychology; I would not assume that I have anything to add to them. Many wonderful words have been written about the Christian faith and what the work of Jesus on the cross means for us today, by people more theologically qualified than me to write them. So why put pen to paper? I realise that I have taught aspects of this material for years, but I have never sat down to put it all together in one place. It is backed up with the twenty-six years of pastoral ministry, and over three thousand hours of client work; I have had the privilege of seeing this material change people's lives. I have to be honest and say that I have had opposition from people who believe the only help you need is the Holy Spirit, to stand by faith and believe the old has gone and the new has come. Whatever you believe about counselling, I hope you will catch God's heart, God's heart for people, ordinary people like you and me.

Experience has also been my teacher. I have sat for hours, listening to Christians who have suffered with poor mental health, because of bad theology that has kept them bound up in feelings such as guilt, anger and low self-worth, because they have been told that they should no longer feel them now that they are saved.

If you read this as purely information, you may be inspired by parts of it and bored by other parts. My hope is that you will engage with the process, like a map that can lead you into greater freedom. A map that may take you over tough terrain, but it will be worth it.

I feel it important to encourage you to find someone you trust, maybe someone in church leadership who can walk this journey of self discovery with you, someone who will support and pray for you as you touch buried feelings.

I started my journey as a church pastor back in 1993. I was young and ambitious for the Lord; I had good leadership training and would have said I was confident and prepared for whatever came my way. But 2008 brought massive change, when people with horrifically broken pasts started to come to church, and I felt at a loss as to how to help them. I believed in the power of the Gospel, the good news that sets people free, and that is what we were experiencing. However, at the same time, I was sitting with people talking about such brokenness and traumas, too horrendous to repeat in a book without minimising their stories. I was aware that I felt overwhelmingly inadequate for the task, so I decided to do a basic secular counselling course, which had a massive impact on my own life.

Level 2 training became level 3 and so on, and I am now qualified to level 6 as a clinical counselling supervisor.

I was bought up with statements like, "big boys don't cry" and "stop that crying or I'll give you something to cry for". I learnt how to suppress feelings and just get on. I grew up with the practice of avoiding feelings, because it was seen as weakness to acknowledge any struggles that I may have had. This continued when I came to Christian faith and I now realise, that I carried this attitude right up until I did my counselling training.

My desire to gain some counselling skills to help others, became an unexpected sideswipe that unlocked my life. Over a process of time I learnt how psychology does not have to compromise the gospel, but quite the opposite if we are willing to engage with it. No one finds it easy to touch uncomfortable feelings, so we end up avoiding or distorting feelings to make things feel more comfortable for ourselves. But if through these following chapters you will open your heart, then big change can come for you.

My hope is that I can write a few words that can open people's hearts to greater inner healing and wholeness. Surely more freedom is good for everyone.

Chapter 1

God desires truth in the inner being

Psalm 51:6 the Message Bible
"What you're after is truth from the inside out. Enter me, then; conceive a new true life."

John 1:14
"The Word became flesh and made his dwelling among us. We have seen his glory, the glory of the one and only Son, who came from the Father, full of grace and truth."

It can be so hard to acknowledge truth. What happens when truth is uncomfortable? Don't we tend to distort it, compromise it, or just avoid it altogether?

As Pilot said to Jesus, "What is truth?" (John 18:38). The reality is that all too often truth becomes relative, truth is what you want it to be, we make truth comfortable, you have your truth and I have mine. We take our stand upon our own truth, often with great conviction, even declaring that we are standing on the word of God.

Some will insist that the truth John is talking about is abstract from us and purely talking about Jesus, the Son of God, the saviour of the world, dying for the sins of the world etc. Of course they are all true and so amazing. Jesus said,

John 8:32

"If you hold to my teaching, you are really my disciples. Then you will know the truth, and the truth will set you free."

And in verse 36

"So if the Son sets you free, you will be free indeed."

If the Son sets you free, wow, free indeed! However, these truths were never meant to be truths claimed in some positive self-help manner, unrelated to any relationship to, or being a disciple of Jesus.

The important thing is how the truth of Jesus touches the depth of truth within our own souls. We need to let Him in. It's deep but amazingly liberating.

Oswald Chambers, the great old preacher of the late eighteen hundreds said:

We can only be used by God if we allow Him to show us the deep hidden areas of our own

God desires truth in the inner being

character. It is astounding how ignorant we are about ourselves! We don't even recognise the envy, laziness or pride within us when we see it. But Jesus will reveal to us everything we have held within ourselves before His grace began to work. How many of us have learned to look inwardly with courage?[i]

The deepest feelings of pain and brokenness as well as joys, live in the depth of our souls, and the truth is that the Holy Spirit wants to make His home there. As scripture says, "Jesus came full of grace and truth," (John 1:14) it does not matter how difficult, or bad the truth may seem to us, there is always enough grace to cover it. Grace, like balm on a wound, will minister to the deepest of hurts and offences of the soul, if we allow Him in, in truth.

"Romans 10:17 Consequently, faith comes from hearing the message, and the message is heard through the word about Christ."

God's Word of truth, releases faith in the heart of the hearer to stand on, but it is dependent upon the seed being planted in the right kind of soil. The right kind of soil stands for the good and noble heart.

When people with this kind of heart hear the word, they retain the word. The seed planted in them will bear the fruit because they persevere by the faith that accompanies the word (Luke 8:15)

Conclusion

Our Father desires truth and integrity from the heart and soul.

Standing on the truth is more than just speaking truth.

When we are open to God in truth, then the truth of God's word will penetrate the deepest parts of our soul and bring restoration through faith.

Prayer

As I start this journey of self exploration, please show me Lord where I have distorted the truth to avoid uncomfortable or painful feelings deep within me. As I sit with you in this place of new awareness, as I open my heart to you, help me to face the truth, trusting your love and grace to bring healing and restoration.

Encouragement

One coping strategy to avoid hard truth is to rush past it quickly, so try not to rush it, God is not in a hurry, give God time to help you process the

God desires truth in the inner being

journey. Journal the changes, those light bulb moments, life changing revelations will come.

COURAGE TO FEEL

Chapter 2

Biology - what we know

We know scientifically that the emotions and body are inseparable. Every cell in our body has a memory. What happens in the mind and emotions can have a massive impact on the body, and vice versa. Though there is still a lot not known about the brain, there is so much more we now do understand around brain development, memory, fight, flight or freeze, hormones, and the parts of the brain that are responsible for how we work. There has been a lot of research and debate from different experts in the world of neuroscience, so this is by no means an in-depth study of the brain, but an attempt to bring out a few thoughts from my own study of what the experts say, that impact us now and can be helpful to understand.

Let's take Hypothetical John. John is fifty years old, a Christian for ten years, loves worshipping God and has an inconsistent relationship with Jesus. He is serving the church, attending lots of meetings and generally doing reasonably well. He still quietly struggles with alcohol. On a monthly basis he finds himself binge drinking and feels so guilty because of his Christian values. He feels shame and guilt because he feels that he continues to let God down. His drinking became a real issue after his wife left him for another man. It was a painful time that really hurt in the depth of his being. He has times now when she returns to his memory which stir up the emotional hurts and pain. Years later his Christian friends are telling him to forgive her and move on, even telling him that God cannot forgive him if he doesn't.

What is happening inside John? Has John forgiven her or is he still harbouring unforgiveness towards her even though years have passed?

Some Bible teachers say he is now a son of God, he needs to renew his mind and forgive her once and for all.

Often things are given spiritual explanations, when it can be helpful to understand the very natural ways in which human beings work.

We will come back to John but let's talk about Hypothetical Jane. Jane has suffered with depression for twenty years, has often thought about ending it all, and still self-harms with a razor blade cutting her arms and legs where no one can see. She is locked in guilt and shame because Christians have told her that Christians don't need to take anti-depressants. Jane was sexually abused by her mother's boyfriend for three years starting at the age of twelve. She is now forty and still struggling with these horrific symptoms, she feels like a second class Christian because she has been made to believe that she needs more faith.

Thousands of Christians sit in churches as broken souls. It does not have to be traumatic experiences that got them there. It is the man who becomes a workaholic to please a father who never told him that he was proud of him, it is the middle aged woman who still believes she is not worth anything, because she could not compete with her elder sister who became the university graduate; she remembers her mum saying, "Why couldn't you be like your sister?" We all carry wounds in the depth of our souls whether we like it or not.

Let's get back to John. When John went through the breakup with his wife, the area of the brain that plays a key part in the sensory areas of understanding emotional experiences, is called the orbitofrontal cortex, this is where Johns emotional vocabulary and capacity to identify feelings are processed. The Hypothalamus is the part of the brain that regulates body temperature, some metabolic processes, and governs the automatic nervous system. The Hippocampus is a component of the limbic system, and plays a part in memory and emotion.

COURAGE TO FEEL

The Amygdala is the emotional centre of the brain, when stimulated it would induce feelings such as anger, fear etc, it is the fight or flight part of the brain.

Because John's brain could not make sense of the traumatic feelings he was experiencing, it triggered a stress response. John's Hypothalamus is struggling to keep his system balanced. This part of the brain then sends out a signal to provide extra energy for John to meet the crisis, by producing the stress hormone Cortisol. When Cortisol is raised it sends out a signal to the rest of the body, including the immune system, to stop what it's doing and focus on the crisis at hand. John is now working from the (Amygdala) fight or flight. The Hippocampus tells the Hypothalamus that the crisis is over and to switch off the Cortisol. The Cortisol is then reabsorbed back into its receptors, or dispersed by enzymes, and the system is back at rest. If stress persists, and high levels of Cortisol remain in the body over a long period of time, it can affect other parts of the body. Firstly in the brain it can affect the Hippocampus, the part of the brain that tells the brain to switch off the Cortisol. Secondly the Amygdala gets excited by Cortisol, and remembers this stressful situation in readiness for the next time that a woman hurts John, ready to spring into action. The logical Hypothalamus says, "I can't manage with this prolonged stress, all of these organs are out of control, I can't stop them, I had better keep away from women."

To make it simpler, John hears a record on the radio that triggers a memory of a time with his wife, that brings back feelings that are remembered in the body. John feels intense feelings that make him feel angry and even depressed.

Jane smells the sweat of a man walking by her in the street and has a panic attack, she freezes because she is overloaded with Cortisol and is now in fight, flight or freeze mode. The Amygdala has taken over in a matter of seconds, because her body remembers the smell of her mum's sweaty boyfriend abusing her when she was a child.

The reality is this. For John and for Jane this has nothing to do with the lack of faith or unforgiveness. This is their bodies working normally in accordance with the experiences of their past. Even if we were to say the past is dealt with spiritually, it does not stop the body reacting normally to stimuli that triggers the fight or flight response.

Because John does not know how to process those feelings, John avoids them by the overuse of alcohol. Jane gets a measure of control by cutting herself, externalising the internal pain with a razor blade. We all find our ways of coping with stress in our bodies.

COURAGE TO FEEL

I have sat with many Johns and Janes over the years and seen massive change when they realise that they are not ill, and they are not mad, but their bodies and brains are working normally to stimuli.

It is now widely agreed that increased levels of Cortisol, particularly in childhood can have a massive impact on the development of the Hippocampus, the part of the brain that helps regulate the stress hormone Cortisol.

So what can be done for John and Jane? Do they have to continue to live like this? People may go to a doctor and get a diagnosis. Psychopathology is to understand symptoms of the mind and give a diagnosis. From my perspective as a psychotherapist, the diagnosis is nothing more than a name for a group of symptoms. It is different to a physical diagnosis, if you break a leg then it is visible and it's a broken leg. When it comes down to the brain or the mind, unless there is a proven brain injury, we should approach it differently, being careful that the doctor's diagnosis does not become the very thing that defines us. Everyone has mental health, it is either good mental health, poor mental health or on a scale somewhere in between. My experience has taught me that no matter what our mental health is like right now, by giving the processing part of the brain an emotional vocabulary to make sense of experiences, we will all move on that scale.

Conclusion

We may not have been able to explain why we feel like we do, or we may behave in a compulsive manner, we may even feel shame and guilt, but be mindful that these are more than likely normal human responses to feelings that we want to avoid.

What is important to know, is that things can change with greater self-awareness.

The chemical balance can be addressed, by giving the processing part of the brain an emotional vocabulary to make sense of experiences.

This does not mean that we are spiritually inadequate, or substandard.

Prayer

Thank you Lord for helping me make sense of my mental and emotional struggles. Show me where my past is creating those anxieties and behaviours. Help me to really understand this theory and how it applies to me.

Encouragement

You are more normal than you think you are! Or have been told that you are! Whatever medical or spiritual diagnosis you may have been given, change can come through this process.

COURAGE TO FEEL

Chapter 3

How is it affecting John's & Jane's lives?

John and Jane do not know how to regulate their own feelings, they therefore hide from them. For some this can come through traumatic experiences, and can be very understandable when you sit with their stories. Traumatic events push people to the limits of coping, as explained in the last chapter.

Research shows that some people are possibly more susceptible to diagnosis such as PTSD (Post Traumatic Stress Disorder). For example, in a study of identical twins, where one brother goes off to war and returns with PTSD. When a brain scan was done on this brother, they noticed that he had a shrunken Hippocampus, which might be expected when we understand how the increased levels of Cortisol, and continual high stress, affects the Hippocampus. However, when they scanned the twin brother, who did not go to war, they discovered that he also had a smaller Hippocampus. Though it is not conclusive, and there is much debate over it, it is likely that the damage was done before the twin went off to war. Being unable to regulate feelings, and in particular extreme feelings, have made him more susceptible to PTSD.[ii]

For many people like John and Jane, they may both have had parents who had never been able to regulate their own feelings, so had no chance of helping John and Jane regulate theirs.

Too many people struggle with poor mental health because they have not been taught how to make sense of feelings at an early age, and then spend their adult years avoiding difficult feelings. People can also hide behind their faith to avoid feelings and never live free lives. Addictions and self-medication can become a way of life for many, attempting to avoid or comfort self, rather than dealing with the underlying feelings. The substance that is used soothes the emotional distress, but usually only for a few hours. For example, sweet things and carbohydrates can help release serotonin into the brain, this is why it's called comfort food. Self-medicating is an attempt to restore some internal balance, but the problem is that it leads to addiction as the body craves the substance, and the more you use, the body and brain will need more to get the same effect.

How is it affecting John's & Jane's lives?

We all find our comfort substance, for one it might be alcohol, for another drugs, for another chocolate, for another throwing themselves into work. As Christians we try to find our comfort in God, going to church, or reading the Bible.

But we can still insulate ourselves from those relationships that trigger feelings that we don't know how to regulate.

Is it time to get REAL with how we FEEL?

When we look at the life of Job, I hear the man of faith shout victoriously "The Lord blessed the latter part of Job's life more than the former part." (Job 42:12) After Job had come through the other side, God so blessed him with the best, even greater than he had before. "Wow!" I hear the person of faith say. Hang on, let's stop and take a moment to think... Job lost his business, lost his livelihood – then he lost his kids, they were killed!! Sit with Job for a moment, though the narrative does not say how he felt, just imagine, put yourself in his place, what's he feeling? "But we don't do feelings!" might be our answer – but I suggest that when we read the narrative of Job's life and circumstances, Job did do feelings!

Abraham faced the facts that he was as good as dead in his body, but he did not waver in unbelief and continued to trust that God was able to do what God had promised. (Romans 4:19-20) Can you imagine what Abraham felt when God told him to sacrifice his son Isaac in Genesis 22? Facing the facts and trusting God do not have to be in conflict, quite the opposite, in fact not facing the facts causes greater conflict. It could be argued that if we do not have those difficult facts, then do we actually need faith. It seems that both fear and faith give perspective to the facts. Facts will ultimately be contextualised by our view of the world or our view of God.

Our lives can change if we stop hiding, face the facts, and start trusting. To know that it is alright to be honest with our feelings. There is a way back for John and Jane, and there is a way back for you too.

Did you ever wonder why God asked Adam where he was, when Adam was hiding in the garden after he ate the fruit? (Genesis 3:10) As if God didn't know where Adam was!! Have you ever thought that maybe God wanted Adam to know where Adam was, and to come out of hiding? God knows where we are too. He wants us to know where we are, and to come out of hiding. Is it time to walk into freedom?

Conclusion

There is a way to get past those feelings that have stopped us, even debilitated us from reaching our potential.

The internal conflicts that we feel when we can't face feelings, will bring symptoms of

How is it affecting John's & Jane's lives?

depression and anxiety, as well as physical symptoms of lack of energy and low motivation.

The need to self-medicate to bring internal balance, often ends up being our greatest enemy.

It becomes a daily fight just to do the most ordinary things.

Prayer

Please show me Father how I have been hiding from myself and you. You see my behaviours and coping strategies, help me to start facing the facts, and trust you for change.

Encouragement

If you will, let's go on a journey to freedom. It might not be easy and even sometimes painful, but is it time? We only have one life to live and like Job, the best is yet to come. Do we have an expectation that our loving Father wants us to live free from the chains of our past?

COURAGE TO FEEL

Chapter 4

What it is to be human?

"Gen 1:26 NKJ. *And God said, Let us make man in our image, after our likeness: and let them have dominion over the fish of the sea, and over the birds of the heavens, and over the cattle, and over all the earth, and over every creeping thing that creepeth upon the earth. 27 And God created man in his own image, in the image of God created he him; male and female created he them.*

Gen 2:7 And Jehovah God formed man of the dust of the ground, and breathed into his nostrils the breath of life; and man became a living soul."

So, God made man in God's own image as a "living soul". There seems to be a lot of debate around whether we are made in God's image as a living soul, or whether it is just our spirit that is made in the image of God. Some would strongly say that the soul is of this world, and the spirit is the pure part of us that is of God, that sin resides in the soul and therefore we should avoid anything to do with it, and

that the Holy Spirit connects with our spirit so that's where our focus should be.
Before we go too far it is worth pointing out that Jesus had a soul, spirit and body, and in doing so showed that there was nothing inherently sinful in them, since he was without sin? (Hebrews 4:15)

Yet we know that we have been infected by the sinful nature. (Romans 5:12) Let's try and get a better human understanding of our present condition.

John Ortberg writes *"We live in a world that teaches us to be more concerned with the condition of our cars, or our careers, or our portfolios than the condition of our souls. Maybe because a dent in a soul is more easily concealed than a dented car. Maybe because a dented soul is harder to fix. After a while, the dents pile up, and they stop bothering us. We hardly notice. One dent more isn't going to make much difference. The keeper of your soul is responsible for its dents. You are the keeper of your soul.[iii]"*

Soul, (psuche (ψυχή): "the natural life of the body", "the seat of personality", "the part of man that perceives, reflects, feels and desires", "the seat of appetite",

What it is to be human?

"The language of Hebrews 4:12 suggests the extreme difficulty of distinguishing between the soul and the spirit, alike in their nature and in their activities. Generally speaking, the spirit is the higher, the soul the lower element. The spirit may be recognized as the life principle bestowed on man by God, the soul as the resulting life constituted in the individual, the body being the material organism animated by soul and spirit...[iv]"

"Superficiality," said Richard Foster, "is the curse of our age. The desperate need of the soul is not for intelligence, nor talent, nor yet excitement; just depth. This is the cry of one of the great soul songs of the Psalms: "As the deer pants for streams of water, so my soul pants for you. . . . Why, my soul, are you downcast? . . . Deep calls to deep in the roar of your waterfalls." The soul is the deepest part of you. It is so deep that there are parts to my soul I cannot seem to understand or control. This is why writers in the ancient world, not just in the Bible, would often address the soul in the third person, in a way they would never do with the will or the mind or the body. There is a depth to your soul that is beyond words.[v]"

The tendency is to want to formulate what is spirit, what is soul and what is body, however I am not sure that this is even possible. Soul, spirit and body are all separate aspects of man that cannot be separated.

One very misquoted scripture is Hebrews 4:12-13

"For the word of God is alive and active. Sharper than any double-edged sword, it penetrates even to dividing soul and spirit, joints and marrow; it judges the thoughts and attitudes of the heart. 13 Nothing in all creation is hidden from God's sight. Everything is uncovered and laid bare before the eyes of him to whom we must give account."

I have heard people teach their point of view, that God wants to separate our souls from our spirit. But that is not what it is saying at all. The context is entering God's rest and having confidence in our great high priest, who is Jesus. It is saying that nothing is hidden from God, the word of God can search between the deepest parts of us, it gets right down between joints and marrow, soul and spirit, it searches out and reveals sin and attitudes that lie hidden, untouched, and even avoided and denied.

Conclusion

My soul is me, my personality, my soul is in touch with God and loved by God, He heals my soul, He refreshes my soul, my soul delights in Him. I can feel anguish in my soul, hurt and pain can reside in my soul, and my hope in Jesus is an anchor to my soul. My soul shall one day be liberated from this body of sin and spend eternity with the Lord. John says, "I pray that your soul is getting along well" (3 John 1:2)

How is your soul today?

Prayer

Father, would you please meet the deepest needs of my soul. As I open my heart to you, please forgive me if I have been shutting you out by avoiding these feelings.

Encouragement

Keep it simple, you can be honest with God, He is not looking for perfection, He is looking for a relationship.

COURAGE TO FEEL

Chapter 5

What it is to be spiritual?

Spirit, pneuma (πνεῦμα, 4151) (Taken from the Strong's Concordance Bible App). primarily denotes "the wind" (akin to pneo, "to breathe, blow"); also "breath"; then, especially "the spirit," which, like the wind, is invisible, immaterial and powerful."

We cannot argue with scripture as it does define a difference between soul and spirit, as we see in 1 Corinthians 2:10, and in John 3:6.

Without a doubt our rebirth as children of God is a spiritual rebirth, we might say that our spirit has been brought into life through the Holy Spirit of God OR we, as a living soul, have been brought into life through the Holy Spirit reenergising our spirit (Titus 3:5). For me it can be unhelpful and over complicated to attempt to formulate it, the bottom line is that my soul is brought to life through spiritual regeneration, my soul can only magnify and honour the Lord through spiritual rebirth. (1 Corinthians 12:3.) The important thing is that we acknowledge that moving from darkness to light, from death to life, happens only because of the work of the Holy Spirit within us by grace alone. My soul is me; my spirit is me, and as we will see in the next chapter, my body is also impacted by the work of the Holy Spirit within. (Romans 8:11)

We become new creations (2 Corinthians 5:17), we are awakened to a loving relationship with a Father in heaven because of what Jesus has done for us. We become aware that we are children of God by a revelation given through the Holy Spirit (Romans 8:16), adopted into His family (Romans 8:15), sons and daughters of the living God who has lavished His love upon us.

So what have we learnt? Your soul is you, it can magnify the Lord, and at the same time it can be full of fear, worry, pain, anxiety and ungodly desires. Your spirit is you and can be filled with praise for God (Luke 1:47), it can also be filled with stubbornness (Deuteronomy 2:30), it can be filled with arrogance (Proverbs 16:18), it can be crushed (Proverbs 17:22).

We need to acknowledge that the Bible does not tell us that the human spirit is the perfect holy part of us. The Bible does show that sin is in the soul, yet sin can also be in the human spirit. It is interesting that God tells us to love Him with all of our hearts, all of our souls and all of our strength, and it does not say love Him with all of our spirit!!

What it is to be spiritual?

1Thess 5:23
"May God himself, the God of peace, sanctify you through and through. May your whole spirit, soul and body be kept blameless at the coming of our Lord Jesus Christ"

If the assumption is that the human spirit is the holy part of us, then Paul would not have written "spirit, soul and body kept blameless".

Conclusion

Our spirit is an aspect of who we are, we are spiritual beings.

It can be unhelpful to complicate it or formulate it, we will only end up trying to formulate God, and God cannot and will not be formulated.

We are as a living soul, renewed through spiritual rebirth through the work of the Holy Spirit.

Prayer

Father, please fill me with your Holy Spirit. I cannot do this alone without your power. Holy Spirit, comforter and counsellor, please lead me into truth and healing.

Encouragement

You are a child of God through faith in Jesus. You were designed by God before the world ever began, you are not an accident no matter what you have experienced.

What it is to be spiritual?

COURAGE TO FEEL

Chapter 6

What about the body?

The Greek word "soma", (Taken from the Strong's Concordance Bible App). literally means body as a whole, the Hebrew word "Nephesh" takes it further, used in a variety of ways; including appetite, breath, lust, mind, pleasure.
The new testament uses another word in the Greek "Sarx", translated as flesh or carnal. Sarx is used in various ways such as "the meat of an animal", or "the body as opposed the soul", "human nature and human being".

Let me quote a few scriptures and make some observations.

"Romans 6:11-12 In the same way, count yourselves dead to sin but alive to God in Christ Jesus. 12 Therefore do not let sin reign in your mortal body so that you obey its evil desires"

COURAGE TO FEEL

Romans 7:24 What a wretched man I am! Who will rescue me from this body that is subject to death?

Romans 8:5-8 Those who live according to the flesh have their minds set on what the flesh desires; but those who live in accordance with the Spirit have their minds set on what the Spirit desires. 6 The mind governed by the flesh is death, but the mind governed by the Spirit is life and peace. 7 The mind governed by the flesh is hostile to God; it does not submit to God's law, nor can it do so. 8 Those who are in the realm of the flesh cannot please God.

The body is the mortal part of us that is connected to this realm.

Our body has desires.

Before we knew Jesus, sin reigned in our bodies and we obeyed its evil desires.

When we know Jesus, we are told not to let sin reign in our bodies, not to obey the impulses of the flesh.

If as a living soul I continue to allow myself to follow the impulses of my body, flesh, carnal or sinful nature, I cannot please God and it will only lead to death. But the soul that is not slave to the sinful nature, is free to live the life that is pleasing to God.

Paul tells us to examine ourselves (2 Corinthians 13:5), he also tells us to test our own

What about the body?

actions (Galatians 6:3), and in 1 Corinthians 13:12 the context is love over gifts. He says that when perfection comes, when Jesus returns there will be no more need of prophecy or words of knowledge for we will fully know, however love will be eternal. It also says something that we might miss if we don't look closely, "that as we know fully, we shall also be fully known". I shall be known fully, nothing hidden, no skeletons in the cupboard, no hidden feelings, everything laid bare. I shall know myself fully, let me say that again, I shall know myself fully. I think this is an amazing statement for a man who spent fifty years hiding from himself. I know that we are all still a work in progress, however I have personally experienced the freedom of being able to really look at myself, and to know that I no longer have to hide from me.

We are spirit, soul and body and you can't see the join, I might say I have three parts, but they are all ME singular.

We have concluded that my soul is saved and in communication with God, as is my spirit. But what about our bodies? The body becomes a temple for the Holy Spirit, we commune with God within our own bodies. We offer our bodies as living sacrifices to God and not the sinful nature. Even my body lives with the anticipation that it will be set free from mortality. (Romans 8:23)

COURAGE TO FEEL

When Jesus returns we shall have a wonderful new body (Philemon 3:20). But until then we walk everyday with Christ in us, in this lies the hope of glory to come.

If then we shall be fully known, why not start now? Have the openness to allow the Holy Spirit to shine a light on any area that is still in the darkness of your body, soul and spirit, those hurts and pains that you have been hiding from, unforgiveness, insecurities, attitudes and behaviours. God is more interested in what you allow Him to do in you, than what He can do through you. As already mentioned, there is always enough grace to wash over the worst narrative that you may need to face.

Let me encourage you with one more scripture.

1Thessolonians 5:23-24 May God himself, the God of peace, sanctify you through and through. May your whole spirit, soul and body be kept blameless at the coming of our Lord Jesus Christ. 24 The one who calls you is faithful, and he will do it.

Conclusion

Though we aim to live from a biblical perspective and say that we should be masters of our fleshly desires, and as temples of the Holy Spirit not indulging in the sinful nature, this becomes a lot harder to achieve if the fleshly desires are coping strategies to self comfort, to avoid feelings and experiences that we cannot make sense of.

Prayer

Lord, Please shine your light in the temple of my body and show me what is still untouched. Help me to walk in the light in every area of my life.

Encouragement

There will always be enough grace to cover the deep truths within us.

COURAGE TO FEEL

Chapter 7

Wrong use of Scripture

I have no problem with agreeing to disagree, I don't feel the need to fight my corner. I am offering you something that I hope will help give a greater understanding of the subject of counselling and the gospel. One of the things I have had to contend with over the years, and has caused a personal struggle in me, is when people misquote scripture to back up their argument.

Here is one example, quoting

Romans 12:2 Do not conform to the pattern of this world, but be transformed by the renewing of your mind. Then you will be able to test and approve what God's will is—his good, pleasing and perfect will.

I remember back in the early nineties when people said, "You don't use drums or electric guitars in church, it's following the patterns of the world", and then quoted Romans 12:2

COURAGE TO FEEL

The context of this scripture is offering our bodies as living sacrifices, holy and pleasing to the Lord, and not to conform to the patterns of the world. Put another way, offer ourselves to God, to live to honour Him by renewing our minds from behaviours and attitudes that come from the sinful nature. This instruction is a vital principle in living a life that pleases God, and not a hook to which we can attach anything that we don't like. Now people argue about whether the Bible and science are compatible, but just because the Bible does not mention gravity, doesn't mean gravity does not exist. One of the biggest contentions, is when some people say that psychology and the Bible are not compatible, because psychology is following the patterns of the world, and then misquote Romans 12:2, yet they never argue, that you should not see a doctor if you are physically sick. I have yet to hear a sound Biblical argument opposing the study and understanding of the human Psyche.

Another misused scripture is James Chapter 3:14 regarding what is considered the wisdom of God, verses man's wisdom. I have heard it said that helping people using counselling is man's wisdom. If we take another look at that scripture we will see what it is referring to:

"But if you harbour bitter envy and selfish ambition in your hearts, do not boast about it or deny the truth. 15 Such "wisdom" does not come

Wrong use of Scripture

down from heaven but is earthly, unspiritual, demonic. 16 For where you have envy and selfish ambition, there you find disorder and every evil practice.

17 But the wisdom that comes from heaven is first of all pure; then peace-loving, considerate, submissive, full of mercy and good fruit, impartial and sincere. 18 Peacemakers who sow in peace reap a harvest of righteousness."

As we can see it has nothing to do with the practice of counselling people with their emotions, or the brokenness of their pasts, or sitting with people and holding their pain with them. The scripture refers to attitudes towards one another.

My experience has shown me that many people of faith, avoid their own feelings and prejudices and try to back it up by the use of scripture. I openly admit that in my distant past I was an expert at it. Let me give you an example, I admit to my shame that many years ago, I was massively homophobic. My biblical view of homosexuality is not the issue here. Rather than deal with my feelings around homosexuality I would look for the scriptures to hide behind, and then judge others. But actually, the word "judge" is too weak, a better word would be "condemn", and the stronger the internal feeling that I was avoiding, the stronger the condemnation, in order that I did not have to examine myself. I would have misused James 3 and said that I was standing on the word of God, the wisdom of heaven, yet my attitude was without doubt the wisdom of the world.

I would call counselling the wisdom of God if the motivation is pure, peace loving, considerate and full of mercy.

Conclusion

Whatever we believe must be in harmony with Scripture. It may not conclusively say XYX but XYX must capture the heartbeat of God written in the sacred text.

We don't rely on one single Bible verse taken out of context to back up our own feelings.

It seems to be a generic human condition to avoid really taking a good look at our own emotional soul.

Prayer

Please help me Lord to honour your word and not distort it to suit how I feel. Open my heart to understand what you are saying to me through it.

Encouragement

God's word is powerful and effective, it will complete what God sent it to do (Isaiah 55:1).

Wrong use of Scripture

COURAGE TO FEEL

Chapter 8

Looking back

Have you ever drawn a timeline of your past? A timeline is where you take a piece of paper, draw a line across the face of it, and start to date rough time scales of your history along the line. Starting with the year you were born, add memories that you can remember, for example, first day at school, first school friends, first kiss, first job, first car etc.

Whenever my wife and I walk through a town on a hot day, I always want to walk on the side of the road where the sun is shining on me – the old saying "mad dogs and Englishmen lay out in the midday sun", that's me, whereas Dawn likes to walk in the shade,- sensible! But it made me think about a time line where on one side of the line, I note memories that are the happy sunny side of the street, and on the other side of the line memories that were unhappy, the shady side of the road, starting with my earliest memory to present day. Can I encourage you to have a go? Don't spend more than thirty minutes on it, you can add to it later, just quick-fire things that come to mind.

Before you read further, can I suggest you find a space where you can be quiet, without distraction and have a go.

Done it? Ok. On balance, do you see more things on the sunny side of the street, or the shady side of the street? Don't be surprised if you see more on the shady side of the street. Tests have shown that we have better memory recall when the origin of the memory happened when we were flooded with the stress hormone cortisol. When you look over your timeline are you aware of anything that is specifically emotive for you? Any memories you find yourself rushing past? At what stage of life were those emotive memories? Are you aware of anything you have avoided by not putting it on your timeline?

Ask the Holy Spirit to prompt your conscience over anything that you have purposely missed off.

Be mindful that the world has not changed because you have done this, just how you feel has changed.

Become aware of how those memories can have an impact on your present day feelings.

Let me give you one example that more recently played out in my own life. Two years ago, I was taking my next level qualification, I sent in my first piece of work and it came back to me with feedback written in red. I immediately responded with "I can't do this!!!" I had very strong feelings that were not appropriate for the moment. Sitting with these feelings it took me back to a time when I was nine years old and my school teacher Mr. L. stood me in front of his desk, in front of the whole class, and with red pen in hand began to scribble all over my best efforts... "rubbish, do it again, stay in at lunch time and write five hundred times, I will try harder". I am sixty two years of age, and I can still see his face with handlebar moustache as if it were yesterday, I can even see the shape of his red pen. I wasn't aware these feelings were inside of me until this present tutor touched those feelings with her red writing on my piece of work. This was a feeling that had no place in the present day, yet was as clear to me, as though I were living it again. Rather than avoid these feelings, I was able to feel them and make sense of them, enabling me to overcome the feeling and pass the course.

When we get a stimulus, like a red pen, our brain will always look to our history to give meaning to those stimuli, so remember all feelings are neutral, it's just our history that gives meaning to the feeling in the present moment. The importance of this is not about living in the past, but understanding how that past can impact our present day, and it does so, even if we are not willing to own it. We can bury it, put in a sealed box, but the truth is, it will bite you on the backside whether you like it or not. It will show itself in symptoms like depression, it can show itself in your behaviour, or your emotional allergic reactions. So what now? Don't rush, spend time with your timelines, be mindful of how it feels, this is you, your life and well-being. Invite Jesus in, He understands every feeling, experience Jesus in your feelings rather than running away from them. Let Him bring a freedom to you through your openness to touch those feelings, He will be there ready to sooth your brokenness with His amazing love for you.

Conclusion

Remember it is your history that gives meaning to your feeling, your interpretation of love for example, will be informed by your past experiences.

My past beliefs that I could not excel academically, were informed by a teacher who showed me no encouragement and could not inspire me to achieve.

Sit with those feelings and ask the Holy Spirit to bring healing and clarity, to re-inform how you feel today.

Remember those feelings may not belong in today but have a use by date somewhere in your past.

Looking back

Prayer

Please help me Lord to see myself as you see me, help me to lay aside old beliefs that have shaped me. As I look at my timeline, Holy Spirit will you show me where my past is still impacting my present.

Encouragement

Our history might have shaped our past, but it does not need to shape our future.

COURAGE TO FEEL

Chapter 9

What's in your glass?

When I sit with my clients, I will often take my glass of water, that I have on my windowsill next to me, and explain our lives like this: This glass represents our emotional fullness, the bottom two inches belongs to me, which I need to own and take responsibility for, no matter how hard it is to face. The rest belongs to other people that I carry, and that narrative might be different for everyone. But let me give you an example: Introjects from my dad's great expectations that I would take over the family businesses, were impressed upon me from the age of 14. However, I was thrown into carrying the load at the age of 24, when dad died suddenly. Like many men of his generation he didn't share his feelings, he was not the kind of man to tell me that he felt proud of me. So I spent many hours sinking under the pressure of a position that I was not made for, but still continued to try and make him proud of me, five years after he had died. I remember a time when an uncle said to me that my dad would be proud of me, and I remember the exhilarated feeling I had when he said this. Was this mine to carry in my glass or was it my dad's expectations that I was carrying? I decided this was partly my dad's, his expectations that I was still trying to live up to, and my own internal need for a dad who would tell me he was proud of me. I decided through the process of talking about it, that it was time to empty those expectations out of my glass. I could never be truly me, if I kept living to expectations that block my own emotional growth into being fully me. The fact that Mr. L kept telling me I was rubbish at reading and writing, meant that I didn't read a book from cover to cover until I was 31 years of age. How much of this is mine to own, and how much is due to Mr. L's inability to inspire and encourage me? I was only nine. I may not be the best academic in the world, but feel I am far better than Mr. L. led me to believe, and through talking about it I was able to offload Mr. L's stuff, and now love reading and studying, and even attempting to write a book! I understand now that those feelings do not need to stop me.

How about you? Are you aware of how other people's "stuff" (Oxford Dictionary states "stuff" as a person's belongings, equipment or baggage) has influenced your identity? Things people have said to you that speak more about them, than they do about you. I have sat with the most beautiful people who believe that they are the ugliest, because that's what they were brought up to believe. I have sat with

What's in your glass?

women who were told that sexual abuse was a normal thing and believed it to be love. Some people still live with secrets, because they are carrying the responsibility of other people's stuff. It can only create conflict inside, and a need to avoid painful feelings by self-comforting in some way to try and regulate how they feel, and it does not need to continue this way.

What's in your glass? Please understand that I am not saying it's a time to start attacking the memory of my late father, he was my hero and I know that he loved me very much. There is no such thing as the perfect father, and I need to acknowledge that my dad never talked about his own feelings, so how was he to talk to me and help me to understand mine? The effect it had on me, was that I would continue to avoid my feelings into adulthood. What is important is that I acknowledge it, understand it and validate the truth to move on.

I wonder whether you can look at your timeline and ask questions around whose stuff this really is? Question how it affects you? You are carrying the aftereffects in your glass; do you need to? Is it yours to carry? Yes, it may hurt, but hurt might be the right feeling to feel, acknowledge and validate it rather than bury it. You carry wounds in your soul that Christ wants to heal, invite Him in, you are worth more than this.

Do you still worry about what people think of you? Do you have an internal need to please others? How about living to unrealistic ambitions and goals to please others? Are you able to tell others how you truly feel, or do you bottle it up through fear of what they might say? Do you feel a responsibility to rescue everyone else from their feelings? When you look at your timeline again can you see how you have become the person you are? Can you understand?

We end up wearing masks to create a persona that is miles away from who we really are, and often just to please others because we feel that we won't be accepted if we don't.

What would it be like to be truly loved for who you are, you are special, unique, there is only one of you in the universe?

God Loves YOU, in fact He loves YOU so much He wants YOU free and whole. Free from the effects of your past, to live as the person He designed you to be, and the life He planned for you to live.

Conclusion

Have you been holding on to things that belong to others?

Do you carry a belief system that is based on what you have been taught to believe?

What's in your glass?

Do you have internal conflicts which lead to such symptoms as depression and anxiety because you live to the false expectations of others?

Have you lost any sense of true self, so you wear masks to meet the need for every different situation?

Do you feel like you are the least important person in the room?

You are special, the only one like you, valuable to the core.

Things can be different; God wants you to be whole and free.

Prayer

As I look at my timeline Lord, would you show me what is mine to carry, and what belongs to others that I have been carrying. Help me to make sense of it all, and clear those blockages that have stopped me from reaching my full potential.

Encouragement

You may be in a deep place right now, but be mindful that the world has not ended, nor has it changed because you have new awareness, it is how you feel about it that will be changing.

COURAGE TO FEEL

Chapter 10

The Mighty Dot

I use this illustration to help explain to others what is happening internally:

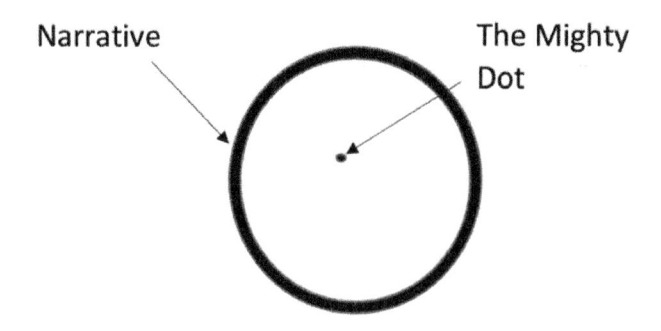

Narrative → ◯ ← The Mighty Dot

The Narrative
This is the story line of our life, everything written on our timeline and more, everything that has ever been said to us, and everything that has been done to us, everything that should have been said and wasn't, the things we have said and done to others. The joys and the losses all in the narrative of

our past experience. Now, whilst it is important to validate our experiences, this is not the main issue that we are working with. Let me take you to the Mighty Dot.

The Mighty Dot

This is the epicentre of our emotional self, the soul with all of its hurts and pains, as well as its joys and pleasures. This Dot is so tiny, but if it were to get touched, it could grow to the size of the moon in less than two seconds flat. All of those feelings stored there, untouched, just waiting for the right stimulus to touch it and bang! We need to run to avoid the feelings, or distort the narrative to make it a feeling we can cope with. The problem is not so much the narrative but how we feel about the narrative. We make it our aim to avoid touching that Dot, we risk assess every conversation to protect it, we will avoid places and people that get too close to it. Insecurities, depressions and anxieties are a few of the symptoms that trying to control that Dot can cause.

Can we start to be honest? If I were to ask you what you think so far? Your answer may not be based upon some theological viewpoint but based on how you feel. Sit with that thought. When we listen to the preacher talk about money, our reaction is more likely to be based upon how we feel about it, and we then find those scriptures that back up our feeling, rather than seeking what the Bible actually says about the subject. Am I right? If your Dot has grown as we talk about this, you may be wanting to throw this little book in the bin! – If you do, be aware that it is your feelings that are driving you to it. Whether you like it or not, your Dot grew and you had to protect yourself, you probably used your biblical views to justify why you want to throw it away.

It all starts with your senses, taste, touch, hearing, seeing and smell. Your senses create a stimulus and your brain says, "what does this mean?" It then looks into the information stored in the different parts of your brain from your past experiences, to give meaning to the stimulus. Your feelings, that belong to twenty years ago, find their way into the present moment. Stimuli can trigger that Dot to grow so fast that it feels like you are reliving the narrative. That's your brain and emotions working normally. You may not be understanding why you are feeling what you are feeling, and that creates internal conflict.

Sometimes feelings are just the accumulation and overflow of many stimuli. You can even feel the aftereffects of stimuli three days later, when the reason for the feeling has passed. The important thing is to know that the world will not end if we touch feelings. We need to grow in emotional wholeness and emotional maturity, be responsible for our own feelings, and not blame everyone or everything for them. They are our feelings and they are important to acknowledge.

Remember Hypothetical John? His wife left him, and he had made alcohol his go-to comfort. John is an adrenalin junky. He has done bungee jumps, he's jumped out of aeroplanes with a parachute strapped to his back, yet he avoids talking to women. He panics if a woman shows an interest in him. His boss is a very confrontational woman, always chasing him for information. John doesn't understand why he is feeling depressed at work, he has been to see the doctor and been prescribed anti-depressants. Let's stand back and look at this, John can control the feelings to jump out of a plane, yet really struggles to control his feelings around women. From the outside, you might say that does not make sense.

How about the man or woman who can ride a motor bike at one hundred miles an hour, but struggle to say a few words at their daughter's birthday meal? How about the man or woman who has earnt a black belt in martial arts, but has a panic attack when seeing a spider running across the floor? Or the man or woman in business who deals with millions of pounds worth of turnover a year, but struggle with anxiety around family gatherings? How about the Pastor who stands up in front of people every week to preach or teach from the Bible, but struggles with anxiety in a small group? You have to

The Mighty Dot

hear the backdrop story of everyone's life to make any sense of why they are struggling, but if they are not willing to go there then they will just keep reliving those cycles of feelings and behaviours, often making the same mistakes just to avoid their Dot.

Understanding feelings is to ask whether it is an appropriate feeling for now. For example, if I am standing in the middle of the motorway with lorries coming towards me, then fear and anxiety is what I should be feeling in that moment. However, if I am standing on a chair and screaming because there is a spider in the room, then that is a feeling out of control. The truth is that I am safe, I just don't feel safe. Another thought to bear in mind, is that if I am standing in the middle of the motorway with lorries coming towards me, it will not be the feelings of fear and anxiety that will kill me! The lorry will, but the feelings won't. No matter what is happening your feelings will not hurt you.

What I am about to say can be hard to accept when you have been the victim, however if you have been the persecutor you might like this. Jesus died for the sins of the world, it does not say he died for the sins of the church, or the Christian, it says the sins of the world, (John 3:16) which means everything in your narrative has been paid for. It is the Dot that Jesus is interested in, the healing of your soul, think about it, your narrative is forgiven, finished, is it time to get REAL with how you FEEL.

Conclusion

The narrative of our life is a story that needs to be heard and valued.

We have feelings that are informed by our past.

The most important thing to hear is the pain in the depth of our soul, our Dot that grows out of control when touched.

We may have avoided it all of our life, but it still bites us when we least expect it.

It causes allergic emotional reactions whether we like it or not, it comes out in the way we speak to people, it will even come out in the way we pray, it will influence the decisions that we make.

We might think that we are spiritual enough to contain it, but we are not, no matter how much faith we can muster.

Prayer

Help me Lord to make sense of my feelings, not to avoid them. Help me to see how my feelings impact my responses. Show me the difference between feelings that are relevant, and not relevant, for the here and now.

Encouragement

Feelings do not need to hold us back; the world won't end if we touch them.

COURAGE TO FEEL

Chapter 11

Person Centred Counselling

Let me start this chapter by asking you not to have a knee jerk reaction if I mention the word Psychotherapy, Humanistic, or something similar. Please hear me out, as sometimes we are in danger of throwing away the baby with the bath water.

Carl Rogers, one of the founding fathers of Person-Centred Therapy, suggested that in every human being there is a driving force which he called the Actualising Tendency. This driving force would ensure that we would strive to grow towards the best possible fulfilment of our potential. This lives in harmony for me with how God made us in His image, we were born to thrive, we were born to rule over creation.

What happens when this Actualising Tendency gets blocked? What happens when our environment has not allowed us to grow in a healthy direction? What happens when our only choice to fit into an environment, is to become a person that does not reflect our true identity? Being internally confused, not knowing who we are, hiding from painful feelings, self-comforting and self-harming to avoid or escape the pain, leaves us with an internal conflict but with no understanding of how to express it, and in some circumstances, not being allowed to express it, even if we knew how. The pain of this internal conflict can become so deep that it causes symptoms such as depression, anxiety, lack of self-worth and stress. Person Centred therapy works with six necessary and sufficient conditions, three of them are core conditions which I feel are central both to therapy and my Christian faith.

Non-Judgemental
Empathy
Congruence

Non-judgemental: No matter what clients tell you from their own narrative, a Person-Centred therapist never judges. Remember the narrative has been paid for. Are you glad that God does not judge you? I know there will be a day of judgement when all will stand before the judgement seat of God (2Corinthians 5:10) and be judged not only for what we have done, but even things we have thought and said. But that's His domain. We need to be mindful not to get caught up in judging the person when we hear their narrative. Our judgement will be fed by our own prejudice, our prejudice will be our way of avoiding our own feelings, which makes it impossible to ever hear the needs of the broken soul inside the person we are trying to help. Remember that people's behaviour is a response to avoiding their own Dot.

Empathy: When I ask people what they think empathy is, the response often is "the ability to walk a mile in another person's shoes", it's a cliché, but most people do not know in practice what that means. Empathy is not a skill to be learnt, but an experience of having the emotional availability to hold the pain of another. How can we genuinely have the emotional availability, if we don't have the capacity to hold our own pain? Put another way, if I spend all of my time avoiding my own pain, then how can I be free to genuinely hold another's, without my pain influencing the moment. Maybe God wants to speak into the moment, but how can I tell the difference between God's voice, and my own pain influencing my thoughts? I cannot be free to hold the pain of another without judging, if I don't own my own. I could go a step further and say, what right do I have to encourage others to talk about their pain if I am not willing to face my own? Isn't that hypocritical?

Congruence: We all have a real and a false self, the self that we want the world to see, and the self when we are alone. Incongruence is when these two do not match. The need to wear a mask shows that there is incongruence, and will always cause inner conflict. God desires truth in the inner parts, He desires that we be fully congruent, at one with God, self, and others. To be open and free to be the special people that we are, without the need to hide from God, self, and others.

It's common when speaking with people, particularly those close to us, to find that they will want to make things better and rescue us from our feelings. But this is not what we need. We need to face up to our feelings without flooding or re-traumatising, to be able to touch those difficult feelings and remain in control of the inner Dot.

My experience has taught me that if I can offer a space where people can experience non-judgemental empathy, they will feel able to look at the brokenness of their own lives. My belief is that if I offer this space to my clients then God is in the room. After all, they are the ingredients that God used to save me thirty years ago. He did not judge me, He empathised and held my pain, yet He wanted truth and integrity, and still does.

What would happen if through talking we could shift some of those blockages? Our Actualising Tendency would drive us into a healthy future. We may all start at different points depending on our histories, but we will all have that drive within our DNA, bearers of the image of God.

I have been asked if this little book is for Christians or non-Christians? I believe both can benefit, it is a book about loving and accepting people. It is a book about helping people find emotional wholeness and better mental health, undoing some of the damage that was done either through early life or difficult or traumatic events, enabling people to grow. I have sat with many people who have no Christian faith and seen this information help them find new levels of freedom in their daily lives, but I do believe that ultimate freedom can only be found through faith in Jesus Christ, and the counsellor of all counsellors – the Holy Spirit.

Everybody needs to experience really being heard, valued and validated. I believe it's how people would have felt when they talked with Jesus 2000 years ago.

Can you remember the story of the Samaritan woman at the well? (John 4:1-30) She was a non-Jew, a person outside of the community of God. Jesus had a conversation with her and exposed the truth of her life, he could see exactly how she had lived, and yet never judged her. The language was full of grace and acceptance as he preached the gospel of how to be saved, and then interestingly told her that the kind of worshippers God desired, were those who worship in spirit and truth. Non-Judgemental empathy and truth modelled in the ministry of Jesus. It then goes on to say "Then, leaving her water jar, the woman went back to the town and said to the people, Come, see a man who told me everything I ever did. Could this be the Messiah?"

Can you see how Jesus works? Counselling does not conflict with the Bible, but goes hand in hand with feeding the hungry and helping the poor and marginalised. Jesus valued people.

Conclusion

Empathy is having the emotional availability to hold the pain of another.

If we feel judged, we will never be open to share what is going on for us, but if we don't feel judged and we experience genuine empathy from another, then we can start to trust enough to share our deepest pains.

We don't need rescuing from our feelings by people telling us everything will be fine, we need a safe space to touch those feelings in order to move on.

If we have been struggling to move on, then finding the right Person-Centred Therapist might help to make sense of what we have been experiencing, move some of those blockages and release us to thrive.

Jesus exposes the truth in our lives, and then tells us that living in truth is central to our worship.

Prayer
Thank you Father that you do not judge me and you hold my pain, but you do help me to face the truth.

Encouragement
Jesus already knows where you are and what you are struggling with, and He is in your healing.

COURAGE TO FEEL

Chapter 12

Relationships

Let's start with the subject of needing to feel in control. Anyone who cannot control their own emotional world, will have to control their environment in order to feel in control. They will need to control their marriage, their office or workplace, they will need to control their children, control the finances, it's never ending. Let's look at a few examples.

Marriage/Partners/Relationships

I have sat with many failing relationships over the years, and there is one common theme every time, and this is the lack of communication. They do not know how to talk. People who have been together for many years, have never been able to be open with each other. I see insecurities fuelled by assumptions and presumptions of what the other one is thinking and feeling. They send texts to one another with hidden meanings between the lines, or they agonise over the sending of a text because they know that their partner will always be interpreting what they think they mean between the lines. They can never actually say what they feel for fear of what the other will think. They both have a narrative of a past, that they bring into the relationship, and they both, more importantly, have a Dot that they are trying to protect.

So, let's take a look at Hypothetical Fred and Ginger. Fred cannot remember a time when he wasn't watching his mum getting drunk as a young boy, mum was always absent for him, he could never talk about how he felt, he learnt to cope in a very hostile environment as mum brought different men home to stay for a while. How does a young boy like Fred cope through this? He grows up with a sense of loss, a feeling of need of a mother he never had. He feels that it's all his fault, he believes he is inadequate and unworthy of being loved. It is sad to say that stories similar to this are far too common today. Fred is now thirty-two years old and been married to Ginger for seven years. Ginger is on her second marriage. Her first marriage failed because her husband was engaging in adulterous affairs, and blamed her. If only she could have been prettier or thinner, she might have been able to keep her husband's interest.

Can you imagine what these two people are storing in their Dot. Imagine how Ginger touches Fred's Dot when she goes out with the girls and comes home drunk. Fred's Dot grows so fast that he pushes her away, he passively aggressively goes quiet and gives her the silent treatment, he doesn't even realise why he does it, he only knows it hurts, which in turn touches her Dot, and she thinks he will now go off with other women. She grovels to him through fear of losing him. Blaming each other for how they feel, and both feeling out of control, neither of them are aware that their own subjective beliefs and their unspoken feelings, are destroying their own lives and their relationship.

Can you see it? Can you see how, if we don't own our own stuff, we will avoid the pain of our own Dot by transferring the feelings onto our partner. Texts get sent fuelled by the Dot; the Dot interprets the hidden subjective meanings of others. Ours may not be as extreme as Fred and Ginger, but we might recognise the process.

At Work

Are you aware of the dynamics within your office or work environment? How about the manager who has to lord it over the office to keep control of his own feelings? Pressured by targets, he transfers his feelings of stress and anxiety on to others in the office, rather than owning his own Dot. Staff members press the button of his Dot, and rather than be responsible for his own feelings he avoids them. He may have lots of stuff going on at home, pressures financially, pressures of teenagers not behaving in the way he would want them to, in fact no one is behaving how he would want them to. He doesn't do feelings; he was brought up that way. He has so much stuff crammed into a box, untouched and under pressure, so much so that he lives from fight or flight instinct. He's lost any sense of self, and everyone else experiences him through the lens of their own Dot. The manager becomes the bully, and we feel like the victim, we feel the pressure because we are not able to see that it has nothing to do with us, it's his stuff, not ours, yet somehow we end up carrying the responsibility of his feelings in our glass. But remember, if we don't know what is our stuff we cannot know what is his.

Maybe we struggle with being told what to do by someone in authority, or struggle with feedback or correction. It pushes the button of our Dot and the feelings from our history come flooding into the present moment. We either find a place to burst into tears or we internalise it and bury it, or we get angry and blame our boss for how we feel, or we will take it home and transfer it onto our wife/husband/partner, kids or the dog. One subjective world meeting another subjective world. Can you see it?

Relationships

Your Children

If you have ever watched the film "Hook", there is a moment when Robin Williams who plays Hook is annoyed at his ten year old son on the plane, and says, "stop behaving like a child" and the son responds with, "but I am a child" The father could not cope in that moment with his own feelings, he blames his son for how he feels. This is an allergic reaction that caused a response, that pushed all of the responsibility on to his son, to take control of the moment.

Respect is often expected just because we are the parent, when actually respect is earned, but it's perhaps not how we were brought up. In my generation, when our parents said "jump," we said, "how high?" We might not have liked it, but we did it, and now our kids are not behaving how we think they should, and oh how that causes our Dot to grow quickly! We tried not to become our dad, but we realise we are becoming him anyway. All of those feelings from our past bottled up, never talked about, that come out in the way we bring up our kids.

Maybe it's time to break the cycle, have you ever taken time to stop and really listen to your kids? Help them to understand their own Dot, to be in control of their own feelings. Let them know it's right and acceptable to feel things, so they can live openly with a great expectation that they can achieve great things in their lives, and fulfil their potential without the blockages that we have had.

In my early days of parenting, I can say that I was guilty of telling my kids how they should feel, based upon my own inability to touch my own feelings. I spent most of my time telling them, and not enough time listening to them. Through over exercising my autonomy, I did not encourage them early enough to exercise their own. Don't get me wrong, I am so very proud of them, and am hopeful that they haven't had to struggle with the blockages that I had. Getting back to the point, I know we need a balance, but if my chastising my kids came out of my own frustrations because I was avoiding my own feelings, then I've missed the point.

This is not a lesson on parenting, there are many great books out there that can help with that. All I am trying to do is show you what will happen if we keep avoiding that which is inside, at the very core of us.

The Church

I would like to turn your attention to a narrative that played out in the Acts of the Apostles. First of all, Saul who became Paul has a massive experience of the risen Lord Jesus. He knew what it was like to be given a second chance. (Acts 9) Barnabas the great encourager went and sought Saul out and took him under his wing, and they begin a ministry together with the help of John Mark. John Mark was a young cousin to Barnabas (Col 4:10). John Mark's mother was Mary, who opened up her home in Jerusalem for a church group that was led by the Apostle Peter (Acts12:12). John Mark became a close companion to Peter. (1Peter 5:13). This is the backdrop to what happens next.

Saul and Barnabas along with their young helper were released to embark on a missionary journey. (Acts 13:5) In verse 13 it says that John Mark left them and returned to Jerusalem. FF Bruce suggests that perhaps he had not reckoned on the more extensive journey into the highlands of the province of Galatia, on which Paul and Barnabas were about to embark.[vi] Though it does not say, it is apparent that Paul felt abandoned, or deserted by John Mark (Acts 15:36-end). Paul and Barnabas carried on the hard mission with great opposition, planting and establishing churches.

Jump forward to Acts Chapter 15, Paul wants to revisit the newly planted churches to see how they were getting on, and to encourage the believers. This would be a different kind of mission, revisiting possible success stories, catching up with people who already loved and appreciated them. Barnabas wanted to take John Mark with them, however, Paul still holding the wounds of being abandoned by John Mark, had a sharp disagreement with Barnabas that broke up the team, and they both went their separate ways.

This is Paul who had experienced second chances, who preaches on love in 1 Corinthians 13, and how the hand cannot say to the foot "I don't need you" in Chapter 12. He writes in Ephesians of how God has pulled down the walls of division, yet Paul has built a big one here.

I would like to ask some questions and suggest some possibilities.

- Did Paul base his relationships solely upon their usefulness to the cause?
- Galatians 2:13, suggests that the nature of Paul and Barnabas's relationship had changed. Had Paul outgrown the need for Barnabas? Had they grown apart in their theology? Did Paul feel that Barnabas was holding him back, and this issue with John Mark was only a part of Pauls overall issue. In other words, Paul not wanting to take John Mark might have little to do with John Mark.
- It seems that Paul did not value the restoration of John Mark to the team, and Paul still held offences.
- Maybe Paul did not always control his Dot.
- May be if Paul saw John Mark to have given up, deserting the hard ploughing in the last

missionary journey, then he didn't deserve experiencing the fruit of the labour.

- Paul had a pattern of people who were once useful to his ministry, deserting him. I cannot help but wonder whether that was as much to do with him as with them! (2 Timothy 9:18)
- In such urgent times did Paul want "yes men" around him, and maybe his Dot grew when people did not agree with him?
- It is likely that John Mark had gained some real stature, both in character and ministry under the encouraging hand of Barnabas his cousin.
- Interestingly Paul writing to the church at Colossae, acknowledges that John Mark was again a useful helper to his ministry.
- Paul wrote some of the most beautiful and challenging scriptures on love and unity (Ephesians 3 and 4), and also the eye cannot say to the hand I don't need you (1Corinthians 12:21). I cannot help but wonder whether Paul's attitude sometimes did not measure up to his own teaching.
- Paul was human, he did not float around on spiritual clouds and was not always led by the Spirit, but sometimes was led by his feelings.

God takes a group of people that often have nothing in common but their Christian faith. They may see a great vision together, working with different gifts to serve the local church. They may all have a good understanding of scripture, and even agree to disagree on certain passages. But how do they deal with conflict, when their own Dot gets pushed, when feelings cause a reaction that creates a breakdown in relationships, like Paul and Barnabas. Theology often doesn't take centre stage in those moments, but feelings do. James understood this when he wrote in James 4:1-2

"What causes fights and quarrels among you? Don't they come from your desires that battle within you? 2 You desire but do not have, so you kill. You covet but you cannot get what you want, so you quarrel and fight. You do not have because you do not ask God."

Let me paraphrase that for you: what causes those fights among you is your internal struggles with yourself.

Too many times, I have seen people leave church because they are not willing to deal with their own emotions. They blame the leaders for not caring, they will say they don't like the music, or they feel left out and even blame Cyril in the corner that gets right up their nose. They go from church to church, and in every church there is a Cyril in the corner, but they never ask if the problem is inside of them. They are trapped by feelings that they want to avoid. They can't integrate into the life of the church, unless they get a group of people around them that

Relationships

will just agree with them, rescuing them from what they feel, without upsetting or challenging them.

They will not get involved because a feeling will stop them, in fact many times they do not make Godly decisions because feelings stop them. They may not acknowledge it, they may even spiritualise it, but if they are ever to be honest with themselves, it is usually the feelings that they want to run away from, that motivates their decisions.

Some spiritual people believe that you should not make decisions based on feelings, but then make most of their decisions based on their feelings, dressing it up as spiritual, often claiming that God has spoken. I guess it justifies why they make emotional decisions.

So, we have looked at a few illustrations to explain how your emotional button, or your Dot, plays a big role within the different relationships, and the danger of not being self-aware enough to understand the implicit processes within those relationships.

If you were to sit with your timeline again, you might see how those implicit feelings have affected your relationships in the past. Can I encourage you to be honest with your feelings, no matter how painful it may be? How freeing it can be to acknowledge those feelings, to be able to touch that Dot without it growing. To become the person that you are designed to be, and not what everyone else expects you to be. Free from those emotional allergic reactions. Other terms used are "throwing your toys out of the pram", "spitting your dummy out"- emotional allergic reactions that come from nowhere just because your Dot has been pushed. Remember your Dot, this is the emotional centre of your soul and is the part that God is interested in changing, making you whole that you might have the emotional availability to meet the needs of others. Imagine a life without those insecurities, the need to defend or justify yourself, a life where you don't have to please everyone, where the value you place on yourself is not based upon what you do, but who you are, no longer carrying everyone else's stuff in your glass.

Conclusion

Think about Jesus, he wasn't devoid of feelings, in fact because he was able to own his own emotions, he had the emotional availability to truly hold the pain of others. People talking to Jesus would have felt like they were the most important people in the world in that moment. Jesus wept for people. I am sure he would have felt hurt when his disciples abandoned him, but he wasn't filled with insecurities, and did not throw his dummy out of the pram. For Jesus, the one thing he didn't do was let those feelings stop him fulfilling His Father's purpose for His life. Will you?

Prayer
Father help me to become more aware of how my emotions impact my decisions and my relationships. Help me to see how my emotions stop me fulfilling your purposes for my life.

Encouragement
God wants us to have greater emotional intelligence, to be free of feelings that stop us doing His will.

COURAGE TO FEEL

Chapter 13

Stereotypes and prejudice

Imagine you have been invited to a wedding of a work colleague, you know no one else there, and you have been told you can sit anywhere. You are standing looking at the beautifully decorated hall with ten tables, and there is only one chair left at each table. This would cause a panic attack to those who struggle with social anxiety. At table 1, there are two families, beautifully dressed in designer clothes, the kids look immaculate, they are laughing and joking together. Table 2, is a table of bald headed people, they are covered in tattoos and piercings, and that's just the women. Table 3, there are two couples who you know are gay, you have heard your work colleague talk about them. Table 4, the table is already covered in empty beer bottles, and the evening hasn't started yet. Table 5, is a group of five black lads. Table 6, is a group of people who look like they have nothing, scruffy hair and ragged clothes.

We could think of many different types of people, but we risk-assess as we scan the room. We are asking which table would we feel most comfortable at? We pigeonhole people into stereotypes based upon our past experiences, and then we judge them based upon our belief. It's called prejudice. It's how we feel about different types of people.

Before I started my counselling training, I would have said that I was not prejudiced. But the biggest shock was to see just how prejudiced I was. I have already admitted that I was homophobic. A lady dressed a certain way, with lots of makeup, was obviously a girl offering sexual services. Like the young man who had a skinhead haircut, he was obviously looking for trouble, and the young girl driving a tank of a 4x4 must be a daddy's girl, or the young black kid driving his Merc must be dealing drugs.

I grew up near Leicester at a time when Idi Amin kicked Asian Ugandans out of Uganda, and many of them came to the Belgrave Road area of the city. They opened up shops and worked hard to succeed. They took jobs in factories and worked hard to provide for their families. I remember the ill feeling, even anger, that some English people had towards them, it would be too shameful to mention some of the abusive names that they got called. A stigma and stereotype that can still live on today. I had the privilege of working for many Ugandan Asians many years ago, when I was shop fitting.

Stereotypes and prejudice

Many had thriving businesses in Uganda, and were thrown out with nothing but the shirt on their backs. I have since visited Uganda many times, and we regularly visited a place called Murchison Falls, the most beautiful place you could find. Surely it compares with the garden of Eden! Standing at the top of these most beautiful falls, we were told that Amin had thousands of Asian Ugandans thrown to their death over these falls. This brought to reality what my shop keeper friends on Belgrave Road had escaped from. These refugees worked hard to make a new life in a foreign country, and many became very successful, yet many English people filled with prejudice, made them suffer once again.

Every human being has an unseen story to their lives, everyone has their Dot to contend with.

A young man went with us on a trip to Uganda and, on seeing the children, was in tears. He was making statements like, "these kids shouldn't be orphaned like this, these kids are innocent and deserve so much more". The real problem here, was that the experience was touching the pain of his own childhood. Those feelings had been supressed for years, but the moment that he saw those little orphaned kids, his Dot exploded and took him totally by surprise.

Jesus said, "go out into all of the world". Yet if we cannot own our own feelings, then how can we look past the narrative of others to the human being, the living soul that lies beneath. How can we genuinely have empathy if we judge the book by the cover? If we have already made our assumptions, then we are the judge. The homeless man on the street is judged to be a drug addict, yet he lives in the madness of a back story, that would make our hair curl. The person suffering with addiction to avoid his Dot, has an unseen story and is crying out for help; this is not the life he chose; no one chooses to be dependent on alcohol or drugs. If we cannot get past our own prejudices and have a genuine care for the living soul, then how can we be the hands and feet of Jesus.

If we can be so self-aware of our own feelings and able to touch our Dot without avoidance or distortion, then we will be emotionally available to touch the soul of others without judgement. We cannot take people on a journey, if we are not willing to go there our self.

Conclusion

We may not be consciously aware of it, but do we pigeonhole people to protect our Dot? Sit with that thought a while and ask yourself how you feel about that.

Stereotypes and prejudice

Ask yourself why we do that, what makes us uncomfortable?

Do you have the emotional capacity to hold the pain of others, or do your prejudices that protect your own Dot get in the way?

Prayer
Father, show me where I hold prejudice, show me how my prejudice is protecting my Dot and influencing whom I build my relationships with, and those I avoid building relationships with. Please give me greater insight into how my history has created my prejudice.

Encouragement
The greater the self-awareness, and the greater the understanding, the greater we can regulate feelings and receive healing and freedom.

Chapter 14

Free fall thinking

When you get on a number 2 bus from Loughborough it will take you to Leicester via the same route, through the same villages every time. Every 20 minutes, the same route. Thought processes work in the same way. If a thought is triggered, and often a subconscious thought, it will always end up at the same destination.

A few years ago, I was having trouble with my computer, it was working so slowly, that I would turn it on and have my breakfast while it finished booting up. My friend had a look at it and told me that I had too many programs open on my desktop. He said, "all of these programs are running in the background, you need to close them down". I thought that was an amazing illustration to explain how we work. Our narrative, with all of the suppressed feelings, are running like programs in the background of our subconscious. Like long playing records, they go around and around and never switch off. The fight or flight is always on high alert. A trigger, which could be a smell for example, will impact our present moment with feelings. Often it will happen when you are in what I call "free fall thinking", away with the fairies, zoned out of the present moment. Leave your brain to do what it will do, and it will always do it. Back to the same point of feeling really low, and you don't know how you got there. You do now. It's a form of meditation that runs in the background of our mind and feelings. The Bible tells us to renew our minds, and meditate on the truth of the word of God. We will come to this in chapter 17, but you will struggle to renew your mind when your feelings keep dictating what you should think. Talking about it can begin to bring closure to those areas of your narrative that run in the background, by giving the brain the vocabulary to tell the fight, or flight it is not needed.

Have you ever wished sometimes that you could switch your head off? Round and round, like living on a roundabout. The same roundabout of thinking, trying to find answers to questions, like why did that ever happen to me? I may not be consciously asking myself that question, but it is a question unanswered on the roundabout of my subconscious. Cycles of behaviour keep doing the same old thing, as my brain continually tries to make sense of it. Attitudes and motivations are informed by our past, whether we like it or not. It's what it means to be complex human beings, fearfully and wonderfully made by God, and if we compare ourselves to what

Free fall thinking

God created us to be, we are all somewhat messed up, and there is always room for more freedom in our lives.

Conclusion

It is as if we have been automatically living to an internal script, informed by our past.

It runs like a play list on Amazon music, it never switches off.

Facing those feelings, rather than running away from them, will begin to rewrite the script.

Self-awareness gives us choice as to which bus to get on, or off!

Prayer

Help me to change the meditation of my negative script, for the script You have written for me through your word. Help me to make sense of those feelings that have no relevance in the present; those worries and concerns that have been running in the background for years, that have no place now. Help me to make sense of, and regulate my feelings.

Encouragement

Sit and think how far you have come in such a short time. You are starting to touch feelings, and know that it's ok.

COURAGE TO FEEL

Chapter 15

Start to live

Through our past experiences, we may have been closed down to our feelings and our actualising tendency has become blocked. Being an image bearer of our Father in heaven, has been reduced to bearing an image that reflects our environment. Our perception of the world, has been moulded by the significant relationships that have been in our life. We can be locked into a system where we just go with the flow, keeping everyone else happy at personal internal cost to ourselves, often because our acceptance comes with other people's conditions. Person Centred theory calls this "conditions of worth"[vii], when our value, as well as our sense of being accepted, and even loved, is based upon the quality of what we do, and not who we are. Internal conflicts can cause us to fight with aggressive behaviour, or comply with passive aggressive behaviour.

For my readers who may be struggling to accept what I have been saying, may I ask you a few questions and ask you to answer honestly?

COURAGE TO FEEL

1. How do you feel when people disagree with you?
2. How do you feel when someone of the opposite sex tells you that you are wrong?
3. Do you update your profile picture on Facebook constantly in order to gain likes, and if so, why? How do you feel if people don't give you the feedback you needed?
4. Are you competitive? I wonder why?
5. Is your image, and how you are perceived by others the most important thing to you?
6. Do you bow to peer pressure?
7. When you look at your friends around you, are they people who will tell you the truth? How do you feel about that if they do?
8. Are you able to tell those who are close to you, how you really feel?
9. Are you able to say no?
10. What is your relationship like with your parents, whether they are still here or deceased?
11. How do you get on with your siblings?
12. How about anger or aggressive behaviour?
13. Do you use passive aggressive or patronising behaviour to keep control?
14. How about sarcasm as a way of getting your point across?

Start to live

If you are not sure, then try asking someone close to you to be honest. Sit with your timeline again, and ask where those conditions of worth have impacted you.

In this broken world, mans love comes with conditions. God's love is purely unconditional, let that truth touch your soul. Person Centred therapy works with the central focus of something called "Unconditional Positive Regard"[viii], being genuinely non judgemental, empathic and congruent.

Can a person be in total control of every feeling? The answer is no. However from a biblical, as well as a Person Centred therapy point of view, it is achievable to grow to self-organise, self-regulate, and to put in order and structure feelings, in a way that you can take responsibility for how you feel, no matter what you face. Remember that self-awareness gives you choice.

There has been a lot documented about the Holocaust of the 1940s by survivors and researchers. Victor Frankl. (1973) was an Austrian neurologist, psychologist and holocaust survivor, who demonstrated that no matter what we face, we can choose our responses. He said that the "*human being is a deciding being.*[ix]" One of his beliefs is that between stimulus and response, there is a space. In that space is the power to choose our response. In our response lies our growth and our freedom.

COURAGE TO FEEL

If we can understand and own our own feelings, then we can choose our responses to the environment in which we live.

If anything that has been written so far resonates with you, then talk to someone, start to touch that Dot. Be honest with those feelings, invite Jesus into those feelings, experience Him in the highs and lows of what you feel. Let the chains of old thinking fall away. Move those blockages that have hemmed you in, start to grow again, fulfil that potential. Your story might need to be heard, and how you feel will need to be validated, you can then move forward with greater self-awareness, and again, where there is self-awareness, there is choice.

What happens next is very powerful and you might need courage. The moment you start to experience this internal change, will also bring its challenges to everyone around you. There may be those who don't want you to change. Your change will now need your environment to change to meet the real you, and you might get some kickback from your environment. But what do you do? Be pressed back into the mould that pleases others? And be what others want you to be, because they are more comfortable with the way they have always related with you.

You are worth more than the sum of your experiences, maybe it's time to find the real you, the identity that God made you to have. It may feel like you are swimming against the tide in your present relationships, but you have a choice. Counselling is not something we do when we are sick and want to get better, at every stage of life, talking about our feelings can lead us into new freedoms. Should we settle for just getting through or managing the status quo? The danger is that if we are always avoiding the difficult feelings, then we are likely to miss the beauty of the heights that we can soar to.

It is vital we understand, that what we are feeling in this present moment may or may not be a feeling relevant to this moment, they may be feelings that belong to the past and not relevant right now, they may be feelings that are appropriate and there to keep me safe, or feelings that are inappropriate and out of control.

Conclusion

It is important to be able to understand, make sense of, and validate our feelings.

We do not need to be afraid of feelings, but grow in emotional intelligence.

Feelings do not need to hold us back.

Prayer

Help me to be honest with my feelings, to make sense of them. Give me courage to face the pressures of my environment, to stand up in the image that you have created me to be. I invite you Jesus to come and minister to those feelings that have previously held me back.

Encouragement
Name those feelings, face those feelings, invite Jesus into those feelings, and those feelings will no longer have the power.

Start to live

COURAGE TO FEEL

Chapter 16

Faith and feelings, the railway track

A helpful way to think about feelings and faith is to think of train tracks that run together, held together by big heavy wooden sleepers. Our lives run on these tracks in everything we do. Our destination has been predestined in His love, He has a plan for our life, His perfect will in accordance with His pleasure, to the praise of His glorious grace (Ephesians 1:4-6). If we have been predestined in His love, then not only has the destination got to be a great place to arrive at, but the journey too. Life might throw some tough times at us because we live in a fallen universe, but we are always held in His love.

These truths are one track, the other track is how do we feel about that? For everything that we will face in life, we will have to consider the truth of God's word, and how we feel about it.

We will always have to push through feelings to operate by faith and serve God, but if we are not open to touch those feelings, they end up being too big for us and we refuse to engage with God's purpose because of how we feel. Have you ever heard people say, in the context of a prayer meeting, that they feel that God is prompting them to pray a prayer out loud? They don't do it, and then someone else prays the prayer that they had on their heart. What stopped them? What stops you? Feelings! Probably worry, about what other people might think of you; where does that feeling come from? Have another look at your timeline. Maybe that feeling had a "use-by date" sometime way in the past, yet it stops you now. I am not saying suppress that feeling again, but own it, it won't hurt you, it's just a feeling that had great relevance back then, and it may be good to talk about it, but do you need it now? Understand the feeling. Name it. Invite God into it and sit with Him in the feeling. Invite the Holy Spirit into that feeling and you will find that your weakness will become God's strength in you. Be mindful, open and honest with the state of your soul, and He will lift you up, it's called walking in the light. (1John 1:7) It's called putting on the belt of truth (Ephesians 6:14).

I would like you to consider that God is as much interested in how we live the journey, as He is in us reaching the destination. Put another way, the process with God in all things is as important as the outcome.

Faith and feelings, the railway track

We spend so much time trying to avoid the hard feelings, that we treat God like a microwave. God please change these painful feelings to joy – ping! Done! when in reality God wants us to experience Him in the painful feelings, to know Him, experience the Holy Spirit in the feeling, sit with Him and allow Him to bring restoration to our soul. We will experience a side of God that we will never experience in the joys. He turns our sorrows into joy through a process of time, when we allow Him in.

God speaks out in Isaiah 6, "Whom shall we send?" Isaiah heard this and said, "Send me". God did not say to Isaiah, "I am sending you". Isaiah heard the call and responded. God still calls out now. "Who will go and preach the gospel to the lost and broken, who will go and minister to the poor and sick, who will give their money for the relief of others, who will give their time to sit with the lonely?" The reality of whether we respond or not is often not a faith issue, but a feeling issue. It's how we feel, that will more likely stop us responding to the call of God. Can you see now how important it is to know yourself more fully?

This is something we can accredit to our relationship with Jesus, that it is completely acceptable and right to be fully me, fully accepted as I am? Fully open and in relationship with God. Isn't this the best thing I can offer to God and mankind?

COURAGE TO FEEL

Have you ever thought about Peter? Jesus gave him that name, it means Rock. Where was the rock when he denied Jesus three times? On the third time it is recorded that Jesus looked directly at him (Luke 22:60). What stopped him being the Rock? Feelings! One in particular, - fear. This was a real fight or flight moment, the feeling was too big for him, he could not regulate those feelings in that moment, and he had to run. Jesus predicted it; He knew it would be a feeling too big for him to handle.

So what had changed for Peter at the end of his life, that he could welcome death for Christ? Was it something to do with Jesus restoring his soul, "Do you love me, Peter, more than these?" (John 21:15) Out of his relationship to Jesus Christ, restoration of his soul had taken place. Out of our intimacy with Jesus, we too can know healing to our soul, the Holy Spirit is the counsellor of all counsellors. If we can regulate our feelings through our relationship with Jesus Christ, then we will always be aware that no feeling has to be too big for us. There will always be time between stimulus and response to choose whether we run or stand by faith.

Think for a moment about Jesus, He did not anaesthetise His humanity with His deity, he felt everything and still was able to have that space between stimulus and response, and see the joy that lay before Him and endure the cross (Hebrews 12:2). He felt everything we feel and more, and so

Faith and feelings, the railway track

can empathise with everything we feel. The Holy Spirit, the Comforter can touch the deepest parts of our soul, no matter how deep and painful it might be. Remember there is always enough grace to cover your truth. The apostle talks about us comforting others with the comfort we ourselves have received. (2Cor 1:3-4). As I have said, we live in a fallen universe, God does not send pain our way, it is a symptom of the world in which we live. Firstly, God will not waste the opportunity to reveal more of Himself to us through it, if we are willing to accept and experience it, and secondly, He will enlarge our capacity to help others.

The big question is whether we want to avoid our Dot, and self- comfort in some way, or whether we are open to touch our Dot, and allow the God of all comfort to comfort our souls.

We may never have to go through a death like Jesus, or Peter and many others who have died for their faith, but most of us struggle to choose our response when people offend us because they didn't like our Facebook photo! People struggle to choose their responses, because their feelings are way too big to face, in what seem to be the most insignificant circumstances.

This can change with emotional maturity. Don't get me wrong, we are all a work in progress, being made a little more like Jesus every day (2Corinthians 3:18). However the truth is, that we can never achieve spiritual maturity without emotional maturity.

Conclusion

The truth of the gospel is one train line, and how you feel is the other line, and held together with the structure of a solid timber sleeper. We will look at structure in another chapter, with the importance of order, boundaries and rules. It might be prudent to ask you how you feel about laws and rules? Some feelings have passed their sell by date.

Are we able to be honest with our feelings? Can we regulate how we feel? Have we got the space to choose our responses? Or are we still struggling with feelings that are too big for us?

Prayer

Help me to grow in emotional intelligence, and help me with feelings that are too big for me. Help me to face them, understand and validate them, and help me to move forward with greater self-awareness.

Encouragement

As we grow towards the end of this journey, please keep revisiting the previous chapters until it gets deeper in your understanding. Like peeling

Faith and feelings, the railway track

another layer off an onion, the more you revisit these things the deeper we go.

COURAGE TO FEEL

Chapter 17

Structure, order & boundaries

I don't have a big garden now, but I love to grow some runner beans in a trough at the side of my house. You may know that you need to create a structure, with canes tied together like a scaffolding. If you don't, the plants will be in a pile on the floor and be ruined by the weather.

Jesus said that He is the vine and we are the branches (John 15:1-8), but if we do not have a structure or boundaries as scaffolding, then we will be a mess on the floor, and the fruit will come to nothing.

I see it like this, the structure is those non-negotiable truths of scripture, they stand alone as pillars of strength, backed up by the power of the Holy Spirit.

Let me build a scaffold for you.

John 10:10

"The thief comes only to steal and kill and destroy; I have come that they may have life, and have it to the full".

COURAGE TO FEEL

Isaiah 54:16-17
"See, it is I who created the blacksmith who fans the coals into flame and forges a weapon fit for its work. And it is I who have created the destroyer to wreak havoc; no weapon forged against you will prevail, and you will refute every tongue that accuses you. This is the heritage of the servants of the Lord, and this is their vindication from me, declares the Lord".

Ephesians 1:3-6
" Praise be to the God and Father of our Lord Jesus Christ, who has blessed us in the heavenly realms with every spiritual blessing in Christ. 4 For he chose us in him before the creation of the world to be holy and blameless in his sight. In love 5 he predestined us for adoption to sonship through Jesus Christ, in accordance with his pleasure and will— 6 to the praise of his glorious grace, which he has freely given us in the One he loves."

Psalm 23:4-6
"Even though I walk through the darkest valley,
I will fear no evil, for you are with me; your rod and your staff,
they comfort me. 5 You prepare a table before me in the presence of my enemies. You anoint my head with oil; my cup overflows. 6 Surely

Structure, order & boundaries

your goodness and love will follow me all the days of my life, and I will dwell in the house of the Lord forever."

Wonderful, non-negotiable truths, that have power behind them. Ok, so that's four vertical uprights, but imagine many more, many more of the most wonderful promises of God. Let me give you another, *I was chosen in Him before the foundation of the world to do good works which He prepared in advance for me to do. (Ephesians 2:10).*

Now imagine two horizontal braces tied at the top to hold them together. The first is faith and the second is feelings. Every one of those uprights are true, and for it to be strong we must understand the nature of our feelings, take responsibility for them, gain that space to choose, to seek God for the faith to make those truths non-negotiable. So the pillar of truth is that you are not an accident, but you feel like an accident. The pillar of truth is that Jesus said He would, "never leave you or forsake you", yet you feel as if He has left you. Feelings will negotiate the truth to make it comfortable, whereas Faith will agree with the truth, I hope that makes sense to you.

We need space between the stimulus and response, to allow God to release faith into our soul, to know we are not alone. Without that space we will compulsively comfort ourselves in some way, to bring internal balance to those feelings that feel out of control. We can't find that space to choose, without being honest about our Dot.

In our past, holding firm to the truth, may not have been an option, because feelings were too big for us, or to be avoided. Gods truth was just words, used in a psychological self-help way, and often used to avoid the truth within our soul.

Can I encourage you to find a piece of paper and draw yourself a picture of your scaffolding? Get into the scriptures and find those non-negotiable truths as your uprights, draw two lines across the top and name them feelings and faith.

Let me give you a conversation someone might have with God, that might put it into context and make it practical.

"Father, your truth says that you will never leave me, but right now I feel tremendously alone. It feels very painful, and feels like you have left me. I feel very depressed and I am comforting myself with chocolate, because it is a horrible feeling. Lord you know that usually I would look for that sexual relationship to fill this deep need in me, but Lord I have found this space to ask you to meet me in the deep needs of my soul. To find you in my loneliness. I will sit and wait for you Lord. Father I need faith to get me past this, to stop these cycles of behaviour that have plagued me for the past twenty years, I am at the end of myself in this Lord

Structure, order & boundaries

and I am not looking for my own way out, please meet this internal need in me that comes out of my broken past. I am not going to hype myself up to try and make myself positive, and I am not trying to put my faith in "faith", but trust the God of all comfort to produce faith in me. Please change me from the inside out so that I will not keep revisiting this moment. Let me find growth from this space, so that this feeling will not be too big for me in the future."

Conclusion

Feelings will negotiate the truth to avoid painful feelings.

Regulating how you feel will give space to make a different response to stimuli.

You can break the cycles of behaviour if you can regulate how you feel about it.

Ask Jesus to help you validate those feelings and move on.

Prayer

May I ask you to write your own prayer this time? Hopefully you are at a place where things are starting to make sense. What are those feelings that stop you? Those cycles of behaviour that need breaking? Hopefully you are gaining a vocabulary to communicate to the Lord the truth of where you are, and no longer have the need to hide.

Encouragement

Keep growing in this language of feelings, and you will find new levels of freedom. Like learning any new language, it takes time to become fluent.

Structure, order & boundaries

COURAGE TO FEEL

Chapter 18

Let's bring this to a close

Even though you will continue to be a work in progress, you will begin to see differences in the way you understand feelings. I am aware that you may have only skimmed the surface, and it may have shown you just how stuck you are, and you may need to process this further. Don't feel discouraged if you find the need to read this book again and again, like learning a new language, we don't always become fluent overnight, and if necessary talk to someone qualified to help.

Check List

If you have engaged in this process, you will have been on a very deep journey of self-exploration.

You have understood that God wants absolute truth and openness from your heart and soul.

COURAGE TO FEEL

Both biblically and biologically, you now understand and value the importance of the integration of the whole self.

You will now be beginning to see where those feelings and emotions have been informed by your past.

You will be understanding that you are carrying expectations of others, or projecting expectations on to others to meet your emotional needs.

You will begin to recognise where you avoid uncomfortable and painful feelings, and even project them on to others.

You are aware that you are more than the sum of your experiences, aware of the difference between the narrative and the Dot.

You are becoming more aware of how these things effect your relationships. The subjective world, that never gets communicated except in negative undermining ways.

You will have thought about how you judge people, stereotype and hold prejudice, to keep yourself safe from your feelings.

You will be learning that it is absolutely acceptable to be you, that you do not have to let your environment shape you anymore. You have more self-awareness that gives you space to choose a different response.

Let's bring this to a close

You may already be aware that certain people do not want you to change, they will feel more in control if you do not change.

You will be experiencing the reality of God's love and comfort in the reality of your life, as God the Holy Spirit meets the truth of your emotional soul.

You will be understanding how your feelings can distort and negotiate, the absolute truths of God's word.

You can never achieve spiritual maturity, without emotional maturity.

Finally, I would like to say thank you for engaging with this process. Can I encourage you to mark your achievements and growth in some way, as a reminder of your Courage to Feel?

COURAGE TO FEEL

About the author

Paul is sixty two and has been married to his wife Dawn for forty one years, he has two sons, two daughters in law, and four beautiful grandchildren.
Paul started his working career at sixteen as an apprentice joiner, and continued in the building trade with his own business, until October 2019.

Paul became a Christian in 1991 and moved very quickly into ministry, where from 1993-2019 he pastored the Beacon Christian Centre in Loughborough, Leicestershire, gaining full ministerial status with the Assemblies of God in 2002. In 2008 Paul retrained as a Person-Centred Counsellor, and worked part time in private practice, continuing with his studies to become a clinical supervisor. In January 2020, he made counselling his main focus, and is now working full time counselling, mentoring and delivering training programmes.

Pauls hobbies are being creative on his wood lathe and the occasional game of golf, but he loves day trips out with Dawn on their motor bike.

COURAGE TO FEEL

Sources

[i] Oswald Chambers : My Utmost for His Highest : Our Daily Bread publishing 3rd July 2017 : Page January 12th

[ii] Gilbertson et al : Nature Neuroscience 5 (11) 1242-6 : 2002

[iii] Ortberg, John : Soul Keeping : Caring For The Most Important Part Of You : Zondervan, 2014

[iv] Vines Expository Dictionary of Old and New Testament Words : Marshall, Morgan & scott Publications : 1981

[v] Ortberg, John : Soul Keeping : Caring For The Most Important Part Of You : Zondervan, 2014

[vi] F.F.Bruce : Paul the Apostle of the free Spirit : The Paternoster Press 1977 : Page 163

[vii] Dave Mearns and Brian Thorne : Person Centred Counselling In Action : Sage Publications 2007 : Page 11

[viii] Dave Mearns and Brian Thorne : Person Centred Counselling In Action : Sage Publications 2007 : Page 95

[ix] Frankl, V (1973) The Doctor and the soul : Harmondsworth : Penguin

RECOMMENDED READING

Sue Gerhardt : Why love matters, how affection shapes a baby's brain : Routledge 2004

Peter Scazzero : Emotional Healthy Spirituality : Zondervan

Printed in Great Britain
by Amazon